Teach Your Kids

by Being an Example

THIS IS MOM'S WORKBOOK

Name: _____ Date:_____

INSTRUCTIONS:

Use a page or two any time you want to be a good example to your kids!

BY: SARAH JANISSE BROWN

The Thinking Tree Publishing Company, LLC

StillSmiling.net

IT'S TIME FOR SCHOOL.

Draw a Clock.

What do you do all day?

8:00 AM_____

10:00 AM_____

12 Noon_____

2:00 PM_____

4:00 PM_____

6:00 PM _____

8:00 PM _____

10:00 PM_____

Midnight_____

SCIENCE - NATURE STUDY

GO OUTSIDE AND DRAW SOMETHING :

READING TIME

1. Draw an Illustration from your book.

2. Copy an important paragraph from your book.

TITLE:

AUTHOR:

COPYWORK:

NOTES:

DAYS OF THE WEEK

Things To Do Each Day!

 MONDAY

 TUESDAY

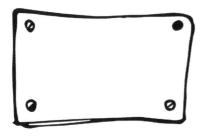 WEDNESDAY

 **THURSDAY**

 **FRIDAY**

 **SATURDAY**

 **SUNDAY**

SOCIAL STUDIES = FACEBOOK

Spend 30 minutes online, and STOP!

What was the most interesting thing on Facebook, Instagram,

Youtube, Google, or Pinterest?

_____

_____

_____

_____

_____

Draw a picture to illustrate

your online experience:

I remember my mother's prayers and they have always followed me. They have clung to me all my life. ~Abraham Lincoln

HOME ECONOMICS & FAMILY RELATIONSHIPS

What was the most important thing that happened today?

_____

_____

_____

_____

_____

FAMILY HISTORY

MAKE A LIST OF IMPORTANT DATES:

Event: Month: Day: Year:

My mother was the most beautiful woman I ever saw.
All I am I owe to my mother. I attribute all my success
in life to the moral, intellectual and physical
education I received from her.
~George Washington

HOME ECONOMICS

THREE THINGS I NEED TO DO TOMORROW:

1.

2.

3.

THREE THINGS I WANT TO DO TODAY:

1.

2.

3.

GOOD NUTRITION

FOODS WE SHOULD EAT OFTEN:

BAD HABITS

FOODS WE SHOULD AVOID:

MATH ~ SPENDING & SAVING MONEY

I Need to buy: Cost:

_____

_____

_____

_____

_____

I Want to buy: Cost:

_____

_____

_____

_____

_____

I can't buy: Cost:

_____

_____

_____

_____

WISH LIST:

SCIENCE - WHAT IS THE WEATHER LIKE TODAY?

_____

_____

_____

_____

_____

_____

What will the Weather Be like Tomorrow?

Draw the Forecast:

SPELLING LIST:

What do you need on a rainy day?

_____   _____
_____   _____
_____   _____
_____   _____

CREATIVE WRITING

Title:

FUN-SCHOOLING IDEAS

Make a list of TEN things that are

both FUN & EDUCATIONAL:

1.

2.

3.

4.

5.

6.

7.

8.

9.

10.

EDUCATIONAL IDEAS
FOR HAVING FUN TOGETHER!

READING TIME

1. Draw an Illustration from your book.

2. Copy an important paragraph from your book.

TITLE:

AUTHOR:

COPYWORK:

NOTES:

CHARACTER CLASS

List three things that you want to

improve in your character or attitude?

1.

2.

3.

Draw a picture of yourself

serving others with a happy heart:

SPELLING LIST:

What words describe good character:

MATH - COUNTING

Make a list of 10 People that you can encourage or pray for this week.

1.

2.

3.

4.

5.

6.

7.

8.

9.

10.

THE SCHOOL OF HAPPINESS:

List 10 things that will bring more happiness into your daily life:

1.

2.

3.

4.

5.

6.

7.

8.

9.

10.

DRAW FOUR LITTLE THINGS

THAT MAKE YOUR FAMILY HAPPY:

MATH TIME!
LET'S COUNT. HOW MANY THINGS
ARE YOU THANKFUL FOR?

_____

_____

_____

_____

_____

_____

_____

_____

_____

_____

_____

_____

WHAT DO YOU NEED

TO DO TO RELAX?

1.

2.

3.

4.

5.

CREATIVE WRITING

Title:

_____

_____

_____

_____

_____

_____

_____

_____

_____

_____

_____

_____

_____

_____

SCIENCE TIME
ALL ABOUT PETS

Good Things about Cats:

Bad Things about Cats:

Good Things about Dogs:

Bad Things about Dogs:

READING TIME

1. Draw an Illustration from your book.

2. Copy an important paragraph from your book.

TITLE:

AUTHOR:

COPYWORK:

NOTES:

MATH TIME
MAKE A SHOPPING LIST:

Item:	Quantity:	Cost:

TOTAL COST:

THINGS I NEED TO BUY:

WHAT IS YOUR FAVORITE SONG TO SING TO YOUR CHILDREN?

Title:

Words:

OTHER SONGS THAT
YOU LIKE TO SING TO YOUR BABIES:

"There is nothing in the world of art like the songs mother used to sing." ~ Billy Sunday

CREATIVE WRITING

Title:

SCIENCE & PHOTOGRAPHY

Nature Photo Scavenger Hunt - Search for each item and when you find it take a picture.

1. Yellow Leaf

2. A Bird or Feather

3. A Smooth Stone

4. Something Red

5. An Insect

6. Something Round

7. Something Tiny

8. Something New

9. Something Old

10. Something Beautiful

SIX INTERESTING THINGS
TO DO OUTSIDE

MATH ~ SPENDING & SAVING MONEY

I Need to buy: Cost:

_____

_____

_____

_____

_____

I Want to buy: Cost:

_____

_____

_____

_____

I can't buy: Cost:

_____

_____

_____

_____

WISH LIST:

_____

_____

_____

_____

_____

READING TIME

1. Draw an Illustration from your book.

2. Copy an important paragraph from your book.

TITLE:

AUTHOR:

COPYWORK:

NOTES:

IMPROVE YOUR MEMORY

Make a list of things to remember:

_____

_____

_____

_____

_____

_____

_____

_____

_____

_____

_____

_____

HISTORY TIME:

Take some time to look at your old photo

collections, albums or scrapbooks.

Show your kids!

SOCIAL STUDIES

WHAT ARE YOUR KIDS DOING ONLINE?

TAKE SOME TIME TO CHECK OUT:

1. Their Search History & Websites Visited

2. Friend Lists (Do you know the friends?)

3. Messages (Look for Bullying and Stalking)

4. Public Photos of themselves (Modest?)

5. Status Updates (Positive & Honest?)

ARE YOU HAPPY WITH WHAT YOU FOUND?

Why or Why Not?

THINGS TO TALK ABOUT WITH MY KIDS:

PERSONAL GOALS

WHAT DO YOU NEED TO CHANGE?

DRAW SIX THINGS YOU WANT TO ACCOMPLISH:

SPRING CLEANING TIPS

GET RID OF CLUTTER.

1. First put ALL the clothing from the entire house into one big pile. Ask everyone to pull out the things that they LOVE to wear. Get rid of everything else. Donate it all.

2. Pull all the books, Movies and CDs off the shelves. Only put away the ones you want to keep. Choose to keep the ones that you enjoy. Donate everything else.

3. Dump all your random junk drawers into one box. Pull out what you use, what you really need, and what you enjoy. Get rid of the rest. Dump the whole darn box of junk.

4. Gather up all the toys an knickknacks that are scattered all over your home. Ask each person to choose the ten things they love the most. Donate the rest.

5. Gather up all your school supplies, games, puzzles, and educational materials. Keep the things that bring joy, spark curiosity and inspire your children to spend time learning.

6. Throw out unused boxes, broken appliances, instruction guides, and outdated electronics.

7. Enjoy an uncluttered home that is easier to clean.

DON'T WAIT FOR NEXT SPING!
AN UNCLUTTERED HOUSE
IS A HAPPY HOUSE!

Only keep the things

that bring you joy!

Donate or throw away the rest.

You don't need those things.

They are clutter. Clutter is bad.

Don't say "I might need it someday."

Give it AWAY! Someone
else needs it now. They
will be happy to find it at
Goodwill for $3.99!

**You don't have to fix,
clean, organize or maintain
things you don't own.**

RELATIONSHIPS

Write About the Power of Forgiveness

_____

_____

_____

_____

_____

_____

_____

_____

_____

_____

_____

_____

_____

_____

GEOGRAPHY

LIST THE PLACES YOU HAVE BEEN

Location: Year:

_____

_____

_____

_____

_____

_____

_____

_____

WHERE HAVE YOU BEEN?

DRAW SOME COOL THINGS YOU SAW:

READING TIME

1. Draw an Illustration from your book.

2. Copy an important paragraph from your book.

TITLE:

AUTHOR:

COPYWORK:

NOTES:

DAYS OF THE WEEK

Things To Do Each Day!

 **MONDAY**

 **TUESDAY**

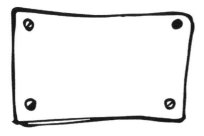 **WEDNESDAY**

 **THURSDAY**

 **FRIDAY**

 **SATURDAY**

 **SUNDAY**

TIME MANAGEMENT

I NEED TO MAKE TIME FOR:

_____

_____

_____

_____

_____

_____

_____

_____

_____

_____

_____

_____

_____

_____

HEALTH & FITNESS GOALS

LIST TEN THINGS YOU CAN DO TO IMPROVE YOUR HEALTH:

1.

2.

3.

4.

5.

6.

7.

8.

9.

10.

DRAW THE FOODS YOU
SHOULD EAT:

CREATIVE WRITING

Title:

_____

_____

_____

_____

_____

_____

_____

_____

_____

_____

_____

_____

_____

_____

_____

SCIENCE:

BAKING EXPERIMENTS

Make a list of things you want to bake.

Find a recipe for each treat. Try One!

_____

_____

_____

_____

_____

_____

_____

_____

_____

_____

_____

BAKING

ILLUSTRATIONS:

MORE

BAKING

ILLUSTRATIONS

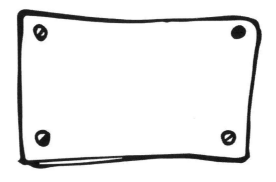

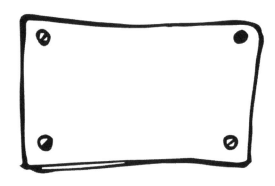

READING TIME

1. Draw an Illustration from your book.

2. Copy an important paragraph from your book.

TITLE:

AUTHOR:

COPYWORK:

NOTES:

WRITING TIME

Write the Words of a Favorite Song

_____

_____

_____

_____

_____

_____

_____

_____

_____

_____

_____

_____

_____

MOM'S SPELLING WORDS:

CREATIVE WRITING

Title:

_____

_____

_____

_____

_____

_____

_____

_____

_____

_____

_____

_____

_____

_____

_____

_____

My Goals:

My Plans:

My Hopes:

THINKING TIME

WHAT ARE YOUR

GREATEST PRIORITIES?

1.

2.

3.

READING TIME

1. Draw an Illustration from your book.

2. Copy an important paragraph from your book.

TITLE:

AUTHOR:

COPYWORK:

NOTES:

Motherhood is a great honor and privilege, yet it is also synonymous with servanthood. Every day women are called upon to selflessly meet the needs of their families. Whether they are awake at night nursing a baby, spending their time and money on less-than-grateful teenagers, or preparing meals, moms continuously put others before themselves.   ~ Stanley

MOM'S THOUGHTS

CREATIVE WRITING

Title:

_____

_____

_____

_____

_____

_____

_____

_____

_____

_____

_____

_____

_____

_____

_____

DAYS OF THE WEEK

Things To Do Each Day!

 **MONDAY**

 **TUESDAY**

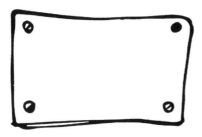 **WEDNESDAY**

 **THURSDAY**

 **FRIDAY**

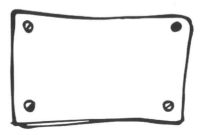 **SATURDAY**

 **SUNDAY**

READING TIME

1. Draw an Illustration from your book.

2. Copy an important paragraph from your book.

TITLE:

AUTHOR:

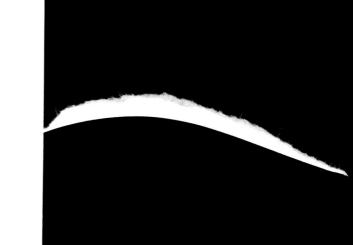

READING TIME

1. Draw an Illustration from your book.

2. Copy an important paragraph from your book.

TITLE:

AUTHOR:

COPYWORK:

NOTES:

"A mother is the truest friend we have, when trials heavy and sudden fall upon us; when adversity takes the place of prosperity; when friends desert us; when trouble thickens around us, still will she cling to us, and endeavor by her kind precepts and counsels to dissipate the clouds of darkness, and cause peace to return to our hearts." ~ Irving

35049016R00058

Made in the USA
San Bernardino, CA
14 June 2016